101(S)
Edition
$10.00
$11.00

CHRISTE LUX MUNDI

Music from TAIZÉ

39 Songs with English Translations

Also available:
G-7101P Assembly Edition
G-7101A Instrumental Edition

GIA Publications, Inc. • 7404 S. Mason Ave. • Chicago, IL 60638 • www.giamusic.com • 800.GIA.1358

Notice

The unauthorized copying of the **words** or **music** of this edition, for any reason whatsoever, is a direct violation of the copyright law for which the person responsible, as well as the institution he or she represents, is subject to prosecution. This includes hand copying, photocopying, even the making of just one copy. To do so is to deprive the creators, as well as the publisher and its employees, of just income.

G-7101 Vocal Edition
ISBN 978-1-57999-692-5

G-7101S Vocal Edition, spiral-bound
ISBN 978-1-57999-693-2

Christe, lux mundi: Music from Taizé
Copyright © 2007 Ateliers et Presses de Taizé.
Published and distributed in North America exclusively by
GIA Publications, Inc. • 7404 S. Mason Ave. • Chicago, IL 60638
www.giamusic.com • 800.GIA.1358

Printed in U.S.A.

Contents

Introduction 4

1. Ad te Jesu Christe (Latin, Ps 25:1–2) 9
2. Alleluia 20 10
3. Alleluia 21 11
4. Alleluia 22 12
5. Alleluia! Slava Tiebie Bože (Russian Orthodox, arr. Taizé) ... 13
6. Beati voi poveri (Italian, Lk 6:20) 14
7. Behüte mich, Gott (German, Ps 16:1, 11) 16
8. Bendigo al Señor (Spanish, Ps 28:6–7) 17
9. Bóg jest miłością (Polish, John Paul II) 18
10. Bogoroditse Dievo 1 (Russian Orthodox, A. Arkhangelski) . 19
11. Bogoroditse Dievo 2 (trad. Russian Orthodox) 20
12. Cantarei ao Senhor (Portuguese, Ps 146:2) 21
13. Cantate Dominum canticum novum (Latin, Ps 96:1) 22
14. Christe, lux mundi (Latin, Jn 8:12) 23
15. Dominus Spiritus est (Latin, 2 Cor 3:17, 6) 25
16. El alma que anda en amor (Spanish, from St. John of the Cross) ... 26
17. Esprit consolateur (French, an expression of Bro. Roger) ... 28
18. Fiez-vous en Lui (French, adapt. from Phil 4:6–7) 30
19. Frieden, Frieden (German, Jn 14:27) 31
20. I am sure I shall see (Ps 27:13–14) 32
21. In manus tuas, Pater (Latin, Lk 23:46) 33
22. In resurrectione tua (Latin, liturgy) 34
23. Jesu, redemptor (Latin, liturgy) 35
24. Jubilate, Alleluia (Latin, Ps 66:1) 36
25. Kristus, din Ande (Swedish, inspired by Jn 4:14) 38
26. Kyrie 19 40
27. Kyrie 20 41
28. L'ajuda em vindrà (Catalan, Ps 121:2) 43
29. Magnificat 3 (Latin, Lk 1:46) 44
30. Nothing can ever (Rom 8:39) 46
31. Que j'exulte et jubile (French, Ps 31:8) 49
32. Qui regarde vers Dieu (French, Ps 34:6) 52
33. Seigneur, tu gardes mon âme (French, inspired from Ps 139:1, 24) ... 55
34. Sit nomen Domini (Latin, Ps 113:2) 56
35. The kingdom of God (inspired by Rom 14:17) 58
36. Tu sei sorgente viva (Italian, liturgy) 59
37. Venite, exultemus Domino (Latin, liturgy) 61
38. Viešpatie, tu viską žinai (Lithuanian, Jn 21:17) 62
39. Wysławiajcie Pana (Polish, Ps 96:1) 64

Indexes (including English translations)
Scriptual and Other References 67
The Liturgical Year 69
Musical Forms 70
Language 71
Title 72

CHRISTE LUX MUNDI

Music from TAIZÉ

Background: The Taizé Community

As many users of this book will know, Taizé is a small village in the Burgundy region of France, which is home to an ecumenical community in the monastic tradition, founded during the Second World War by Brother Roger. In the founder's words, "This intuition has never left me: a life in community could be a sign that God is love, and love alone.... It was essential to create a community where goodness of heart and simplicity would be at the center of everything."

The life at Taizé revolves around prayer, work, and hospitality. Since the 1960s, the hospitality has taken the form of welcoming large numbers of young adults—sometimes several thousand at a time—to stay for week-long meetings. They come to search in the light of the Gospel for a meaning to their lives, through life together in simple conditions, prayer, sharing, and practical work. At the heart of these weekly meetings is prayer with the Community, three times every day.

The "songs of Taizé" were developed in this context, which unites the prayer of a monastic community with large numbers of young people from very diverse backgrounds: what was required was a form of music that was quickly accessible to all, but with the depth and substance necessary to support the daily office of the Community year after year.

What happens at Taizé is continued across the world, as the Community animates an informal series of visits and gatherings of young people, small or very large, which together form a "Pilgrimage of Trust on Earth." The same songs are used at these meetings, which are always undertaken in collaboration with local churches. The young people taking part in this "pilgrimage" have brought the songs of Taizé back to their own churches, where over the years they have become well known and widely used.

The Songs of Taizé

The prayer at Taizé is almost entirely sung, except for scripture readings and very short spoken prayers and blessings. Over the course of the year, numerous different musical forms are used, including hymns, psalms, long or short responses and litanies sung *a cappella* or accompanied by the organ, and certain songs from the Orthodox tradition. However, what is most characteristic is the use of the "songs of Taizé," such as those printed here. These fall into several musical categories, but they have one feature in common: they are essentially composed of short texts sung in harmony that are repeated many times. This element of repetition is closely allied to their meditative character.

The texts are chosen with care: a few words taken directly from the Bible or inspired by a central theme of the Gospel. This enables the songs to play a significant role in the search for reconciliation among Christians that is so important at Taizé: they easily cross denominational boundaries. The meaning of each song can be quickly grasped by the mind, and can then little by little take root in the heart as it is repeated. The songs thus reflect the ancient tradition of repeated short prayers, such as the Jesus prayer of the Orthodox tradition, or the Rosary in the west.

The basic musical forms are simple, but they can be elaborated, for example with solo verses and varied instrumental accompaniments, according to the needs and possibilities of the moment. They are thus very flexible, and can be used by groups of a few people, or even for individual prayer, right through to gatherings bringing together tens of thousands, where they will be sung by the entire assembly supported by a choir and a full complement of solo singers and instrumentalists.

The Story of the Songs

The songs were first developed at Taizé in the 1970s, as the numbers of young people from different countries grew, and the need to find a way for all of them to participate in prayer together became more pressing. The brothers of the Community worked on this with the composer Jacques Berthier, and their collaboration bore fruit in the first canons, and then in different forms of ostinato.

The earlier songs were mostly in Latin. This had the advantage of being a "neutral" language that did not favor any national group; it is easy to pronounce; and the syllables in general have a musical quality that is particularly appreciable in the case of repetitive songs like these. For these reasons, Latin is still frequently used in new compositions. But songs have also been composed in the different languages of the people coming to Taizé, and the range of these languages continues to increase. Though the pronunciation can be a challenge at first, the use of living languages can make the songs closer and more accessible for the different language groups, and more useful for local prayer groups or churches. Furthermore, translations have increasingly been made, so that a song written in one language can be used in another.

Since the deaths in the 1990s of Jacques Berthier and of Brother Robert, his principal collaborator in the Community, the brothers have continued to produce new songs. The prayer of the Community needs both continuity and constant renewal; meetings in new countries create the need for songs in new languages. At present, brothers of the Community compose new songs in the now familiar forms, as well as in developing them and in exploring new directions.

This Collection

The songs of Taizé were first presented to the English-speaking world in the 1980s in *Music from Taizé 1 & 2*. These two volumes were followed in 1991 by *Songs and Prayers from Taizé*, the first book to give English translations for many of the songs, and in 1998 by *Songs for Prayer*.

The present collection contains the principal songs written since then, nearly all composed by brothers of the Community. The contents do not overlap with the titles mentioned above. It is published in three editions: the **vocal edition** contains, as well as the congregational parts, all the solo verses in English. The congregational parts on their own are also available in the **assembly edition**. These two are completed by the spiral-bound **instrumental edition,** which contains the full accompaniments for guitar, organ, and a wide choice of other instruments.

Musical Forms

The musical forms used fall into five main groups (see index on p. 71):

—songs sung by the assembly in continuous repetition. These are either **canons** or **ostinatos**. They may be as short as four bars (*Kristus, din Ande/Jesus, your Spirit in us*), or much longer (*Seigneur, tu gardes mon âme/O Lord, you hold and protect me*). For some of the ostinatos, there are solo verses that may be superimposed from time to time as the assembly continues to sing.

—songs in which the harmonized singing of the congregation alternates with verses that are sung by a soloist, while the assembly sing *oh* or hum on a series of chords. These could be called **ostinato refrains**. In some cases the *oh* is very brief (*Wysławiajcie Pana/Praise our God and Savior*); in others, it is prolonged (*Magnificat 3*). In either case, the assembly should not fall silent. For these, the solo verses are printed out in full.

—the *Alleluias* and *Kyrie eleisons*, which are **acclamations** or **refrains** sung by the assembly between verses of praise or intercession. The assembly sings a long *oh* or hums between each refrain (perhaps sustained, if necessary, by the organ), while the soloist improvises the verses; the chord of the *oh* changes at the end before repeating the refrain. The effect created is unusual in Western music, and it is a powerful one: as they sing the continuous *oh*, the congregation can unite strongly behind the prayers offered, and the different intentions come together without any sense of detachment or individualism. In the case of the *Kyrie eleisons*, it is also possible for the assembly to hum while, instead of sung verses, intentions are offered in a clear speaking voice. For these, no solo verses are printed out, since different psalms and intercessions should be chosen for each occasion, and the exact melodies of the soloists are meant to be improvised. But we have printed, as an example, possible verses for *Alleluia 20* and *Kyrie 19* (#2 and #26, respectively). Further examples can be heard on the CDs *Christe, lux mundi* (for *Kyrie 20*) and *Venite, exultemus* (for *Kyrie 19* and *Alleluia 20*). Finally, this collection includes two versions of the Orthodox prayer *Bogoroditse Dievo*, and the song of praise *Alleluia! Slava Tiebie Bože*. These songs form part of the current repertoire at Taizé, and while they may not always be suitable for use in English-speaking parishes, those who have heard them at Taizé or on the recordings may wish to have the printed music available. The presence of these songs is an expression of trust and of gratitude for the faith and testimony of the Orthodox churches.

Using the Songs of Taizé

Two essentials should be borne in mind, whatever the context in which these songs are used: First, the songs are meditative, and are intended to help open a contemplative dimension of prayer. And second, they are intended to allow the participation of everyone.

Meditative character

The songs are meant to help people *take time* in God's presence. They should be sung for long enough to allow distracted thoughts to calm down and for the words to sink in: each song is typically repeated for about four to eight minutes. (It defeats the purpose of the songs to sing them, for example, only three or four times over.) The number of times does not have to be fixed in advance; but someone—a singer or instrumentalist—should be designated to bring a song to an end and start the next one.

"Meditative" however does not mean "slow and sad," and care should be taken not to let the tempo slow down too much. The spirit of praise always entails an inner decision, and this can be expressed by a certain energy or vigor in the singing. Even the quieter songs can be suffused with this. On the other hand, an over-enthusiasm that races ahead too quickly is also to be avoided. Metronome marks are given to indicate the best tempo for each song.

The songs can be used in many different contexts. On the one hand, they can form the main element of a prayer service, as at Taizé itself or during the meetings organized by the Community.[1] In this case, the other elements will usually be a short Scripture reading, a five or ten-minute time of silence, intercessions and maybe a spoken prayer. (For more specific suggestions, see Other Resources below.)

In other settings, several Taizé songs sung one after the other can be useful in order to deepen a contemplative aspect at particular moments, for example during Communion, or after a reading, or leading into and out of a time of silent adoration. They can also serve as a "bridge," to help people coming in from a busy world to become more still and to orient themselves at the beginning of a service. However, careful thought should be taken before simply using one of these songs instead of a hymn or other worship song during a service of a quite different style: the style might only conflict with the rest of the service.

Outside a church setting, some of the shorter ostinatos and canons can also help to bring moments of recollection and thanksgiving during the day, for example before or after meals, before starting work, in the evening before sleeping. And many people find themselves singing or remembering these songs when alone, during personal prayer, or at other times.

Participation

The *raison d'être* of these songs is to allow everyone to participate: they were not written to be sung by a choir or soloists while the congregation simply listens. Everyone present should sing the melody, and, where possible, the harmonies too. At Taizé, visitors are often surprised at the joy a large congregation with no particular musical training can find, after just a little practice, in singing together in four voices.

If there is a choir, their role is to support the assembly, assuring the harmony of the ostinato or the further voices of the canons. The accompaniment of a classical guitar, organ, piano, or cello plays a similar supporting role. The solo verses may be superimposed as desired while the assembly continue to sing; these enrich the prayer with new themes for meditation. The other instrumental parts add varying melodies and tonal colors, and are superimposed as desired in the same way as the solo verses.

The same song can thus take a variety of forms or levels of complexity, from simple unison singing of the unaccompanied melody at one extreme, to a harmonized version with a full complement of solo voices and instruments at the other. This means not only that the songs can be used for gatherings of widely different sizes, but also that it is possible during the course of a single service to vary the treatment of the songs: one could be sung with guitar and soloists, another unaccompanied, others with different instrumental groupings.

The ostinatos and canons can be sung with the simplest of resources; the ostinato refrains, however, require a certain minimum number of singers and at least one solo voice.

A feeling of spontaneity and freedom should be maintained; but some planning in advance is always necessary. For example, if several solo voices or instruments are used, someone should indicate the different entries and *tacets*. If he or she needs to conduct, this should be done with as much discretion as possible, so as to avoid distracting the assembly.

The harmony should not be left to spontaneous impulse or individual choice: the printed voices should be respected. The assembly should not attempt to make up their own harmonies or new descant voices.

The original language versions are printed here together with the English translations. The Latin songs may be sung in the original whenever desired; the other languages can be used if there are speakers of that language present. It is usually better to avoid singing the different language versions simultaneously. Singing different language versions one after the other, as though they were different verses of a hymn, should also be avoided: this would significantly detract from the meditative character of the songs.

Other Resources

Detailed suggestions for preparing a time of prayer using the songs of Taizé can be found in the book *Prayer for Each Day* (GIA Publications, G-4918, ISBN 1-57999-029-0).
More ideas are proposed on the Taizé website **www.taize.fr**.

Nearly all the songs printed here can be heard, in the original languages, on the two CDs *Venite, exultemus* (GIA CD-529; in Europe T565) and *Christe, lux mundi* (GIA CD-696; in Europe T568). The pages "Learning the songs," found under the tab "Prayer and song" on the Taizé website (**www.taize.fr**), give the possibility of hearing the different voices independently.

---

[1] The Community asks people to avoid expressions such as "Taizé service" which can somehow draw attention away from the really important thing, which is the simple fact of people meeting together to pray.

1. AD TE JESU CHRISTE
I Lift Up My Soul to You

*optional entry

2. ALLELUIA 20

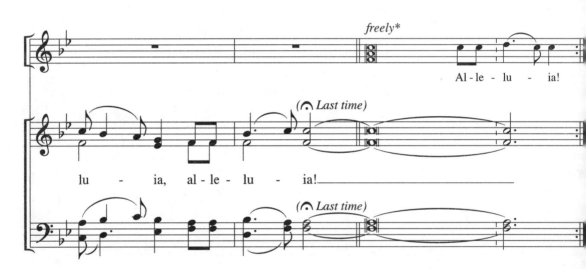

*The cantor may improvise, beginning the phrase on any one of the three notes. The following example may be used as a model.

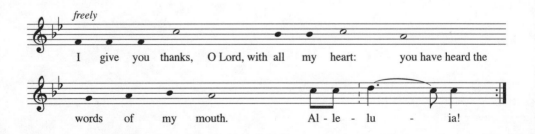

3. ALLELUIA 21

*The cantor may improvise, beginning the phrase on any one of the three notes.

4. ALLELUIA 22

*The cantor may improvise, beginning the phrase on any one of the three notes.

5. ALLELUIA! SLAVA TIEBIE BOŽE
Alleluia! Glory Be to You, Lord

7. BEHÜTE MICH, GOTT
O God, Keep Me Safe

8. BENDIGO AL SEÑOR
I Bless You, Lord, My God

9. BÓG JEST MIŁOŚCIĄ
God Is Forgiveness

10. BOGORODITSE DIEVO 1

O Virgin Mary, you who gave birth to (Christ who is) God, rejoice, highly favored one, the Lord is with you. You are blest among women, and blest is the fruit of your womb: the Savior of our lives, to whom you gave birth.

11. BOGORODITSE DIEVO 2

Bo-go-ro - di-tse Die-vo, ra-dui-sia, bla-go-dat-na-ia Ma-ri-e, Go - spod

s to-bo-iu: bla-go-slo-vie-na ty v že-nah, i bla-go-slo-vien plod tchrie-va

tvo-ie-go, ia-ko Spa - sa ro-di-la ie-si duš na-ših.

12. CANTAREI AO SENHOR
I Will Sing to the Lord

*No third

13. CANTATE DOMINO CANTICUM NOVUM
Sing a New Song to the Lord, All You Peoples

14. CHRISTE, LUX MUNDI
Christ, You Are Light

This page is blank in order to avoid page turns.

15. DOMINUS SPIRITUS EST
Lord and Giver of Life

16. EL ALMA QUE ANDA EN AMOR
Whoever Walks in God's Love

Verses From 1 Corinthians 13:4–7; Psalm 116 *(superimposed on second part of ostinato)*

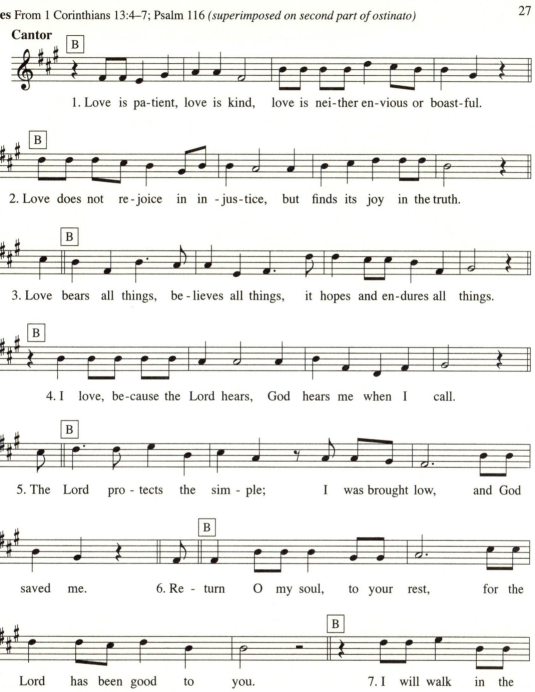

1. Love is patient, love is kind, love is neither envious or boastful.
2. Love does not rejoice in injustice, but finds its joy in the truth.
3. Love bears all things, believes all things, it hopes and endures all things.
4. I love, because the Lord hears, God hears me when I call.
5. The Lord protects the simple; I was brought low, and God saved me.
6. Return O my soul, to your rest, for the Lord has been good to you.
7. I will walk in the presence of the Lord in the land of the living.

Verses From Saint Simeon the New Theologian *(superimposed on second part of ostinato)*
Cantor *freely*

1. Come, true light, Come, life eternal, Come, hidden mystery, Come, Holy Spirit!
2. Come, un-name-a-ble treasure, Come, joy without end, Come, light that never fades, Come, Holy Spirit!
3. Come, our heart's desire, Come, our very breath and our life, Come, our glory, our unending joy, Come, Holy Spirit!
4. Come, make your home in us, Come, live in us until the end, Come, that we may live in you, Come, Holy Spirit!
5. Come, keep us standing, Come, fill us, poor as we are, Come, that we may go from joy to joy, Come, Holy Spirit!

18. FIEZ-VOUS EN LUI
Put Your Trust in God

19. FRIEDEN, FRIEDEN
Peace I Leave You

*No third

20. I AM SURE I SHALL SEE

22. IN RESURRECTIONE TUA
The Heavens and the Earth Rejoice

23. JESU, REDEMPTOR
Jesus, Redeemer

Verses From Psalm 66 *(superimposed on ostinato)*

*Choose either part.

25. KRISTUS, DIN ANDE
Jesus, Your Spirit

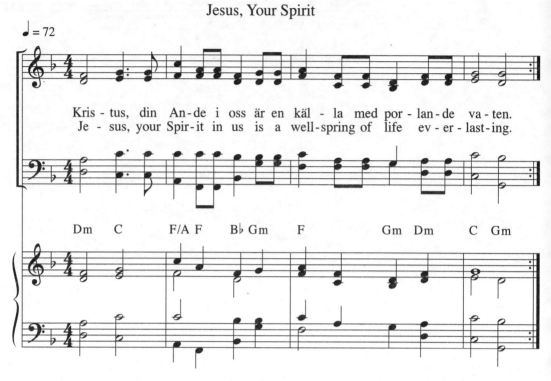

Kris - tus, din An - de i oss är en käl - la med por - lan - de va - ten.
Je - sus, your Spir - it in us is a well-spring of life ev - er - last - ing.

Verses From Psalm 63 *(superimposed on ostinato)*

Cantor

1. O God, you are my God, for you I long, my soul thirsts for you. I wish to gaze up - on you, Lord, in your dwell - ing, be - hold - ing your pow - er and your glo - ry.

26. KYRIE 19

*The cantor may improvise, beginning the phrase on any one of the three notes. The following example may be used as a model.

27. KYRIE 20

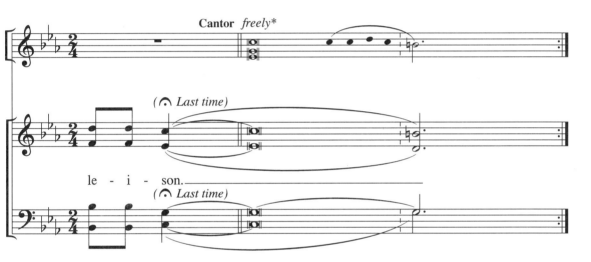

*The cantor may improvise, beginning the phrase on any one of the three notes.

This page is blank in order to avoid page turns.

28. L'AJUDA EM VINDRÀ
I Lift Up My Eyes

29. MAGNIFICAT 3
My Spirit Exults and Rejoices

*No breath

Verses From Psalm 56; Romans 8:31–39 *(superimposed on second part of ostinato)* 47

This page is blank in order to avoid page turns.

31. QUE J'EXULTE ET JUBILE
I Delight and Rejoice

Verses From Liturgy, adapt. *(superimposed on ostinato)*

32. QUI REGARDE VERS DIEU
Look to God and Be Filled

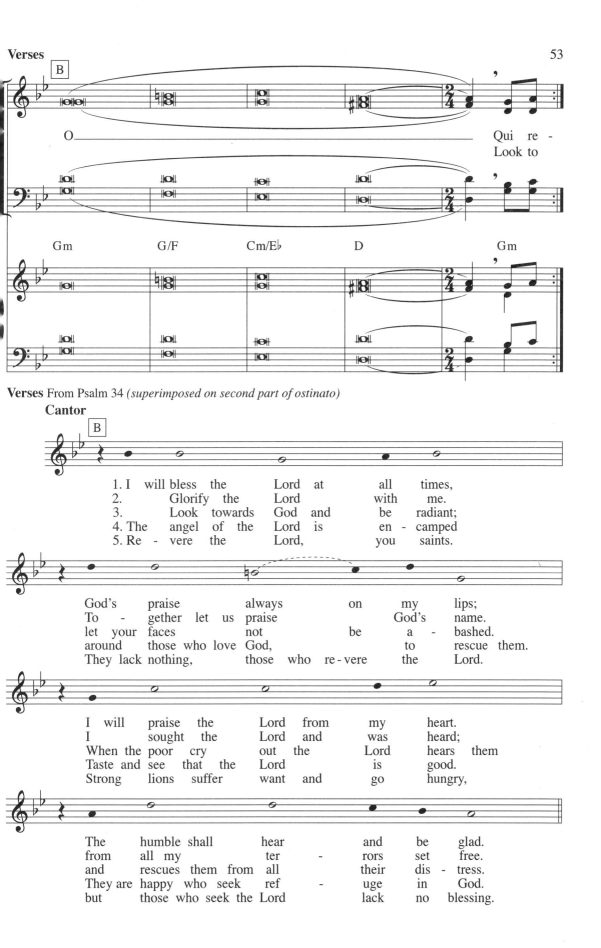

This page is blank in order to avoid page turns.

33. SEIGNEUR, TU GARDES MON ÂME
O Lord, You Hold and Protect Me

Seigneur, tu gardes mon âme; Ô Dieu, tu connais mon cœur. Conduis-moi sur le chemin d'éternité, conduis-moi sur le chemin d'éternité. Sei-

O Lord, you hold and protect me; you know all my heart's desire. Guide my steps along the everlasting way, guide my steps along the everlasting way. O

34. SIT NOMEN DOMINI
Now and Forevermore

Verses From Psalm 113 *(superimposed on ostinato)*
Cantor

1. Give praise, servants of the Lord. Give praise to the name of the Lord. Bless the name of the Lord now and evermore!

2. From the rising to the setting of the sun, give praise to the Lord; praise the name of the Lord!

3. The Lord reigns over the world, God's glory is exalted on high. Who can be compared to our God?

4. God is enthroned in majesty on high but looks down on heaven and earth, to lift up the lowly and to raise up the poor.

35. THE KINGDOM OF GOD

36. TU SEI SORGENTE VIVA
Lord, You Are Living Water

37. VENITE, EXULTEMUS DOMINO
O Come and Let Us Sing to God

♩ = 84

Ve - ni - te, ex - ul - te - mus Do - mi - no, ve - ni - te, a - do - re - mus.
O come and let us sing to God, our hope. God's mer - cy is for - ev - er.

D A/C♯ D G A D   G A Bm Em C   Em Am G D

(🐠 Last time)

Ve - ni - te, ex - ul - te - mus Do - mi - no, ve - ni - te, a - do - re - mus. Ve -
O come and let us sing to God, our hope. God's mer - cy is for - ev - er. O

A/C♯ D G A D   G A Bm   G/E D/F♯ G A^{SUS4} A D

Verses From Psalms 9, 16 and 18 *(superimposed on second part of ostinato)*

Cantor

1. God brought me through, set me free; God saved me, for great is his love.

2. Keep me, O God, my refuge and help. You alone are my joy.

3. Lord, you will show me the path of life. Before your face is fullness of joy.

4. I will thank you, O Lord, with all my heart, I will sing and praise your name.

5. All who know you, Lord, have trust; you never abandon those who seek you.

6. You bring me back, Lord, from the gates of death; I sing for joy, for you have saved me.

39. WYSŁAWIAJCIE PANA
Praise Our God and Savior

Verses From Liturgy, Psalm 136, Luke 1:68–79 *(superimposed on ostinato)*

SCRIPTURAL AND OTHER REFERENCES
The numbers following the titles refer to the song numbers, not the page numbers.

<u>Song Numbers</u>

PSALMS
9:2–3a, 11, 14–15
    Viešpatie, tu viską žinai/ 38
    All my heart lies open to you
16:1–2, 11
    Viešpatie, tu viską žinai/ 38
    All my heart lies open to you
16:1, 11
    Behüte mich, Gott/ 7
    O God, keep me safe
18:20
    Viešpatie, tu viską žinai/ 38
    All my heart lies open to you
25:1–2
    Ad te Jesu Christe/ 1
    I lift up my soul to you
27:13–14
    I am sure I shall see 20
28:6–7
    Bendigo al Señor/ 8
    I bless you, Lord, my God
31:8
    Que j'exulte et jubile/ 31
    I delight and rejoice
34:2–11
    Qui regarde vers Dieu/ 32
    Look to God and be filled
56:4, 5b, 10b, 12a, 13b–14a, 14d
    Nothing can ever 30
63:2a, 3–5, 8–9
    Kristus, din Ande/ 25
    Jesus, your Spirit
66:1–2a, 4–7a, 8–9
    Jubilate, Alleluia/ 24
    Shout to God with joy
95:1, 6
    Venite, exultemus Domino/ 37
    O come and let us sing to God
96:1
    Cantate Domino canticum novum/ ... 13
    Sing a new song to the Lord, all you peoples
    Wysławiajcie Pana/ 39
    Praise our God and Savior
113:1–6
    Sit nomen Domini/ 34
    Now and forevermore

<u>Song Numbers</u>

116:1, 6–7, 9
    El alma que anda en amor/ 16
    Whoever walks in God's love
121:2
    L'ajuda em vindrà/ 28
    I lift up my eyes
136:1–21
    Wysławiajcie Pana/ 39
    Praise our God and Savior
139:1, 24
    Seigneur, tu gardes mon âme/ 33
    O Lord, you hold and protect me
146:2
    Cantarei ao Senhor/ 12
    I will sing to the Lord

MATTHEW
5:3–10; 11:28–29
    Beati voi poveri/ 6
    How blessed the poor in heart

LUKE
1:46–55
    Magnificat 3/ 29
    My spirit exults and rejoices
1:68–79
    Wysławiajcie Pana/ 39
    Praise our God and Savior
6:20
    Beati voi poveri/ 6
    How blessed the poor in heart
23:46
    In manus tuas, Pater/ 21
    Into your hands, O Father

JOHN
4:14, 7:37–39
    Kristus, din Ande/ 25
    Jesus, your Spirit
8:12
    Christe, lux mundi/ 14
    Christ, you are light
14:27
    Frieden, Frieden/ 19
    Peace I leave you

SCRIPTURAL AND OTHER REFERENCES
The numbers following the titles refer to the song numbers, not the page numbers.

Song Numbers

21:17
    Viešpatie, tu viską žinai/ 38
    All my heart lies open to you

ROMANS
8:31–39
    Nothing can ever 30
14:17
    The kingdom of God 35

1 CORINTHIANS
13:4–7
    El alma que anda en amor/ 16
    Whoever walks in God's love

2 CORINTHIANS
3:6, 17
    Dominus Spiritus est/ 15
    Lord and giver of life

PHILIPPIANS
4:6–7
    Fiez-vous en Lui/ 18
    Put your trust in God

LITURGICAL
    In resurrectione tua/ 22
    The heavens and the earth rejoice
    Jesu, redemptor/ 23
    Jesus, redeemer
    Tu sei sorgente viva/ 36
    Lord, you are living water

RUSSIAN ORTHODOX TRADITION
    Alleluia! Slava Tiebie Bože 5
    Alleluia! Glory be to you, Lord
    Bogoroditse Dievo 1 10
    Bogoroditse Dievo 2 11

ST. JOHN OF THE CROSS
    El alma que anda en amor/ 16
    Whoever walks in God's love

ST. SIMEON, THE NEW THEOLOGIAN, 10th century
    Esprit consolateur/ 17
    Consoling Spirit of God

THE LITURGICAL YEAR
The numbers following the titles refer to the song numbers, not the page numbers.

<u>Song Numbers</u>

ADVENT
Ad te Jesu Christe/ 1
I lift up my soul to you
Bogoroditse Dievo 1 10
Bogoroditse Dievo 2 11
Fiez-vous en Lui/ 18
Put your trust in God
Magnificat 3/ 29
My spirit exults and rejoices
The kingdom of God 35

CHRISTMAS
Bogoroditse Dievo 1 10
Bogoroditse Dievo 2 11
Jesu, redemptor 23
Jesus, redeemer
Sit nomen Domini/ 34
Now and forevermore
The kingdom of God 35
Venite, exultemus Domino/ 37
O come and let us sing to God

LENT
Beati voi poveri/ 6
How blessed the poor in heart
Behüte mich, Gott/ 7
O God, keep me safe
Bendigo al Señor/ 8
I bless you, Lord, my God
Bóg jest miłością/ 9
God is forgiveness
El alma que anda en amor/ 16
Whoever walks in God's love
Frieden, Frieden/ 19
Peace I leave you
L'ajuda em vindrà/ 28
I lift up my eyes
Seigneur, tu gardes mon âme/ ... 33
O Lord, you hold and protect me

HOLY WEEK/TRIDUUM
Bóg jest miłością/ 9
God is forgiveness
Christe, lux mundi/ 14
Christ, you are light
I am sure I shall see 20

<u>Song Numbers</u>

In manus tuas, Pater/ 21
Into your hands, O Father
Nothing can ever 30

EASTER
Alleluia! Slava Tiebie Bože 5
Alleluia! Glory be to you, Lord
Cantate Domino canticum novum/ 13
Sing a new song to the Lord, all you peoples
Frieden, Frieden/ 19
Peace I leave you
In resurrectione tua/ 22
The heavens and the earth rejoice
Jubilate, Alleluia/ 24
Shout to God with joy
Que j'exulte et jubile/ 31
I delight and rejoice
Sit nomen Domini/ 34
Now and forevermore
Viešpatie, tu viską žinai/ 38
All my heart lies open to you
Wysławiajcie Pana/ 39
Praise our God and Savior

PENTECOST
Dominus Spiritus est/ 15
Lord and giver of life
Esprit consolateur/ 17
Consoling Spirit of God
Frieden, Frieden/ 19
Peace I leave you
Kristus, din Ande/ 25
Jesus, your Spirit
Tu sei sorgente viva/ 36
Lord, you are living water

TRANSFIGURATION
Christe, lux mundi/ 14
Christ, you are light
Jesu, redemptor/ 23
Jesus, redeemer
Qui regarde vers Dieu/ 32
Look to God and be filled

MUSICAL FORMS
The numbers following the titles refer to the song numbers, not the page numbers.

Song Numbers

ACCLAMATION
Alleluia 20 2
Alleluia 21 3
Alleluia 22 4

REFRAIN
Kyrie 19 26
Kyrie 20 27

CANON
Ad te Jesu Christe/ .1
I lift up my soul to you
Cantate Domino canticum novum/ 13
Sing a new song to the Lord, all you peoples
Jesu, redemptor/ .23
Jesus, redeemer
L'ajuda em vindrà/ 28
I lift up my eyes

OSTINATO
Beati voi poveri/ 6
How blessed the poor in heart
Behüte mich, Gott/ .7
O God, keep me safe
Bendigo al Señor/ .8
I bless you, Lord, my God
Bóg jest miłością/ .9
God is forgiveness
Cantarei ao Senhor/ 12
I will sing to the Lord
Christe, lux mundi 14
Christ, you are light
Dominus Spiritus est/ 15
Lord and giver of life
Fiez-vous en Lui/ .18
Put your trust in God
Frieden, Frieden/ .19
Peace I leave you
I am sure I shall see 20
In manus tuas, Pater/ 21
Into your hands, O Father
In resurrectione tua/ 22
The heavens and the earth rejoice
Kristus, din Ande/ 25
Jesus, your Spirit
Seigneur, tu gardes mon âme/ 33
O Lord, you hold and protect me

Song Numbers

Sit nomen Domini/ 34
Now and forevermore
The kingdom of God 35
Tu sei sorgente viva/ 36
Lord, you are living water
Venite, exultemus Domino/ 37
O come and let us sing to God

OSTINATO REFRAIN
El alma que anda en amor/ 16
Whoever walks in God's love
Esprit consolateur/ 17
Consoling Spirit of God
Jubilate, Alleluia/ 24
Shout to God with joy
Magnificat 3/ 29
My spirit exults and rejoices
Nothing can ever 30
Que j'exulte et jubile/ 31
I delight and rejoice
Qui regarde vers Dieu/ 32
Look to God and be filled
Viešpatie, tu viską žinai/ 38
All my heart lies open to you
Wysławiajcie Pana/ 39
Praise our God and Savior

OTHER
Alleluia! Slava Tiebie Bože 5
Alleluia! Glory be to you, Lord
Bogoroditse Dievo 1 10
Bogoroditse Dievo 2 11

LANGUAGE

The numbers following the titles refer to the song numbers, not the page numbers.

<u>Song Numbers</u>

CATALAN
L'ajuda em vindrà/ 28
I lift up my eyes

ENGLISH
I am sure I shall see 20
Nothing can ever 30
The kingdom of God 35

FRENCH
Esprit consolateur/ 17
Consoling Spirit of God
Fiez-vous en Lui/ 18
Put your trust in God
Que j'exulte et jubile/ 31
I delight and rejoice
Qui regarde vers Dieu/ 32
Look to God and be filled
Seigneur, tu gardes mon âme/ 33
O Lord, you hold and protect me

GERMAN
Behüte mich, Gott/ 7
O God, keep me safe
Frieden, Frieden/ 19
Peace I leave you

ITALIAN
Beati voi poveri/ 6
How blessed the poor in heart
Tu sei sorgente viva/ 36
Lord, you are living water

LATIN
Ad te Jesu Christe/ 1
I lift up my soul to you
Cantate Domino canticum novum/ 13
Sing a new song to the Lord, all you peoples
Christe, lux mundi/ 14
Christ, you are light
Dominus Spiritus est/ 15
Lord and giver of life
In manus tuas, Pater/ 21
Into your hands, O Father
In resurrectione tua/ 22
The heavens and the earth rejoice
Jesu, redemptor/ 23
Jesus, redeemer

<u>Song Numbers</u>

Jubilate, Alleluia/ 24
Shout to God with joy
Magnificat 3/ 29
My spirit exults and rejoices
Sit nomen Domini/ 34
Now and forevermore
Venite, exultemus Domino/ 37
O come and let us sing to God

LITHUANIAN
Viešpatie, tu viską žinai/ 38
All my heart lies open to you

POLISH
Bóg jest miłością/ 9
God is forgiveness
Wysławiajcie Pana/ 39
Praise our God and Savior

PORTUGUESE
Cantarei ao Senhor/ 12
I will sing to the Lord

SLAVONIC
Alleluia! Slava Tiebie Bože 5
Alleluia! Glory be to you, Lord
Bogoroditse Dievo 1 10
Bogoroditse Dievo 2 11

SPANISH
Bendigo al Señor/ 8
I bless you, Lord, my God
El alma que anda en amor/ 16
Whoever walks in God's love

SWEDISH
Kristus, din Ande/ 25
Jesus, your Spirit

TITLE
The numbers following the titles refer to the song numbers, not the page numbers.

Song Numbers

Ad te Jesu Christe . . . . .p. 9	Jesus, your Spirit . . . . .p. 38
Alleluia 20 . . . . .p. 10	Jubilate, Alleluia . . . . .p. 36
All my heart lies open to you . . . . .p. 60	Kristus, din Ande . . . . .p. 38
Alleluia 21 . . . . .p. 11	Kyrie 19 . . . . .p. 40
Alleluia 22 . . . . .p. 12	Kyrie 20 . . . . .p. 41
Alleluia! Glory be to you, Lord . . . . . .p. 13	*L'ajuda em vindrà* . . . . .p. 42
Alleluia! Slava Tiebie Bože . . . . .p. 13	*Look to God and be filled* . . . . .p. 50
Beati voi poveri . . . . .p. 14	*Lord and giver of life* . . . . .p. 25
Behüte mich, Gott . . . . .p. 16	*Lord, you are living water* . . . . .p. 59
Bendigo al Señor . . . . .p. 17	Magnificat 3 . . . . .p. 43
Bóg jest miłością . . . . .p. 18	*My spirit exults and rejoices* . . . . .p. 43
Bogoroditse Dievo 1 . . . . .p. 19	Nothing can ever . . . . .p. 45
Bogoroditse Dievo 2 . . . . .p. 20	*Now and forevermore* . . . . .p. 54
Cantarei ao Senhor . . . . .p. 21	*O come and let us sing to God* . . . . . . .p. 59
Cantate Domino canticum novum . . . . .p. 22	*O God, keep me safe* . . . . .p. 16
Christ, you are light . . . . .p. 23	*O Lord, you hold and protect me* . . . . .p. 53
Christe, lux mundi . . . . .p. 23	*Peace I leave you* . . . . .p. 31
Consoling Spirit of God . . . . .p. 28	*Praise our God and Savior* . . . . .p. 62
Dominus Spiritus est . . . . .p. 25	*Put your trust in God* . . . . .p. 30
El alma que anda en amor . . . . .p. 26	Que j'exulte et jubile . . . . .p. 47
Esprit consolateur . . . . .p. 28	Qui regarde vers Dieu . . . . .p. 50
Fiez-vous en Lui . . . . .p. 30	Seigneur, tu gardes mon âme . . . . .p. 53
Frieden, Frieden . . . . .p. 31	*Shout to God with joy* . . . . .p. 36
God is forgiveness . . . . .p. 18	*Sing a new song to the Lord, all you peoples* p. 22
How blessed the poor in heart . . . . . . .p. 14	Sit nomen Domini . . . . .p. 54
I am sure I shall see . . . . .p. 32	*The heavens and the earth rejoice* . . . .p. 34
I bless you, Lord, my God . . . . .p. 17	*The kingdom of God* . . . . .p. 56
I delight and rejoice . . . . .p. 47	Tu sei sorgente viva . . . . .p. 57
I lift up my eyes . . . . .p. 42	Venite, exultemus Domino . . . . .p. 59
I lift up my soul to you . . . . .p. 9	Viešpatie, tu viską žinai . . . . .p. 60
I will sing to the Lord . . . . .p. 21	*Whoever walks in God's love* . . . . .p. 26
In manus tuas, Pater . . . . .p. 33	Wysławiajcie Pana . . . . .p. 62
In resurrectione tua . . . . .p. 34	
Into your hands, O Father . . . . .p. 33	
Jesu, redemptor . . . . .p. 35	
Jesus, redeemer . . . . .p. 35	